MAJESTIC NIGHTS

Majestic Nights

Love Poems of Bengali Women

Selected, Edited and Translated
by
Carolyne Wright
and co-translators

Companions for the Journey Series: Volume 16

White Pine Press / Buffalo, New York

Grateful acknowledgment is due to the editors of the following publications in which many of these poems first appeared in English translation:
The American Poetry Review, American Voice, Arts & Letters, Black Warrior Review, Boulevard, Calyx, Chelsea, Chicago Review, Cimarron Review, Grand Street, Hawai'i Review, Hayden's Ferry Review, International Quarterly, London Review of Books, Michigan Quarterly Review, Mid-American Review (part of a translation chapbook: *A Few Grains of Sweetness in a Dark Time of Worship*), *Mississippi Review, New England Review/Bread Loaf Quarterly, Nimrod, Partisan Review, Poetry East, Poetry Review* (U. K.), *Prism International, Shenandoah, Sou'wester, SPAN* (USIS-India), *The Toronto Review, Triquarterly, Vallum,* and *The Women's Review of Books.* (Acknowledgments continue on page 105.)

Publication of this book was made possible, in part, by funding from the National Endowment for the Arts, which believes that a great country deserves great art, and with public funds from the New York State Council on the Arts, a State Agency.

Library of Congress Control Number: 2008921650

ISBN: 978-1-893996-93-9

White Pine Press
P.O. Box 236
Buffalo, New York 14201
www.whitepine.org

Table of Contents

To all women of Bengal, especially to the memories of
Srima Radharani Devi
Begum Sufia Kamal
Farida Sarkar
Srima Kabita Sinha
Nasima Sultana
whose words illumine these Majestic Nights

And for Jim, our joy in the River of Time

Majestic Nights:
Love Poems by Bengali Women
in a Time of Transition

One of the most compelling figures from Indian myth and legend is the cowherd girl Radha, pining alone in a forest bower for her beloved Lord Krishna, the dark-skinned god whose sensual exploits among the *gopīs* (cow-herding maidens) of Vrindavan and whose passionate and secret love for Radha have been celebrated in song and story since classical times. In Bengal, the great medieval poet Jayadeva composed his *Gītāgovinda*, the "Love Song of the Dark Lord," in the late twelfth century, and the Radha-Krishna story is still revered today, particularly by Bengalis, both as a romantic ideal and as an emblem of the yearning of the human mortal for union with the Divine. Even in predominantly Muslim Bangladesh, devotional songs and poetry dedicated to Radha and Krishna have a great influence on literature and culture, and references to Hindu lore are frequent in the work of Bangladeshi Muslim poets and writers. Could this be because devotional and ecstatic impulses run deep in Bengali culture—not just among Hindus, many of whom are practitioners of Vaishnava *bhakti* yoga, but among Bengali Muslims, with their traditions of devotional Sufism and its search for union with the Man of the Heart? For Bengalis, it can be hard to talk of romantic love without also touching on spiritual yearning.

But in this era of rapidly shifting roles for women and men in the nations and cultures of the Indian Subcontinent, including Bengal, profound changes in social, political, and economic conditions have altered the ways in which women and men interact with each other, even in the most private matters of the heart. And women's poetry has reflected these transformations. Women have participated in literary activities in Bengal at least since the latter half of the nineteenth century, when, as part of widespread social reforms of the "Bengal Renaissance" movement, young upper-caste and upper-class Bengali men began to demand brides who were educated, and families began sending their daughters to newly created girls' schools or hiring home tutors. Some girls and women even taught themselves to read and write in secret, with the schoolbooks and informal clandestine tutoring of their own brothers or sons. As privileged women became educated and increasingly involved themselves in social service work to benefit their less-advantaged sisters, they started to question many of the socially-sanctioned customs that restricted women's activities and participation in society: *purdah* (the seclusion of women), child marriage, *sati* (the immolation of Hindu widows on their husbands' funeral pyres), and prohibitions against any career but marriage and family.

In this light, the mortal Radha in her bower, pining alone for Krishna, becomes an emblem for the helplessness of women in love under conditions of inequality. Radha knows that her divine beloved can do anything he wishes—he may be off cavorting with one of the other cowherd maidens. The god's behavior becomes the model for that of mortal men, condoned and even celebrated by social as well as religious tenets that compel wives to remain at home, faithful to husbands who can indulge in liaisons with courtesans, and—if Muslim or Kulin Brahmin—are permitted to take as many as three other wives. Perhaps the inequality delineated in this trope is somewhat alleviated by the fact that in some versions of the Radha-Krishna story, Radha is a married woman who breaks from the proprieties of loveless wedlock to devote herself secretly and passionately to the service of her true lord and lover.

Today, educated Bengali women from upper-class and middle-class families serve not only as writers, teachers, and journalists, but as physicians, attorneys, financial analysts, and heads of state. Since ousting a military dictator in 1991, the supposedly backward nation of Bangladesh has democratically elected two women Prime Ministers of opposing parties, Begum Khaleda Zia and Sheikh Hasina Wajed. In fact, one or the other of these women has led the nation for most of the election cycles since 1991. But in Bengali society, nearly everyone is expected to marry and have children to carry on the family, and except for some urban, English-educated elite, arranged marriages are still the norm. Arranged marriages do have certain positive features: they can be a boon for young people too shy or too busy with studies or work to seek for themselves; and in a society with very little dating and virtually no "singles' lifestyle," parents with their children's best interests at heart may make wiser choices of prospective life partners.

Nevertheless, a measure of economic independence gives Bengali women much more say in when and whom they will marry, and veto power over grooms selected by their parents. But millions of other Bengali girls from working class and poor families in remote rural villages and in urban slums are still forced to marry at the age of ten or twelve, sometimes to men the age of their fathers. Others labor in the fields or in sweatshops; some are coerced or tricked into sexual slavery in brothels. Even if they marry willingly, in socially conservative traditional families they may have little control over the course of their lives, little opportunity for self-definition in their community or self-expression in their families.

How do Bengali women love in times of social transition and political upheaval? How do they move from that thrill under the skin and catch in the breath, the first hopes for tenderness and mutual understanding, the disappointment of the failure of early love, the skip in the heart beat to marriage and the warmth of long years together, to the pain of separation in death? How can love flower if the woman has little influence in the choice of a marital partner? These poems look at how Bengali women tell their truths of the heart and mind through the prism of their struggles for equality, opportunity, and recognition in a changing society. The poems follow a subtle trajectory through the stages of love: First Love, Marriage, Separation, Aging and Death, and the ultimate Supreme, Universal Love of which romantic love is an imperfect reflection—not unlike the stages of life through which the human psyche moves, from beginning to end and back to the starting anew of the cycle.

This collection includes work from a range of Bengali women poets, the eldest ones born in the women's quarters of *purdah*-observing, high-caste or high-class families in the late nineteenth and early twentieth centuries. The youngest poet included is Taslima Nasrin, a physician turned dissident writer who now lives in exile in the West because of her unsparing criticism of Bangladeshi Muslim culture, religion, and the religious leaders who, she feels, help to foster the low esteem in which women are regarded in her country. Most of the poets represented here are those with whom I met and whose work I translated while living in Kolkata and then Dhaka for two years each on long-term research fellowships. A few poets—Shamim Azad, Ketaki Kushari Dyson, and Dilara Hashem among them—belong to the Bengali "diaspora": they are settled in the West but still write mainly in Bengali, contribute actively to Bengali literary publishing in their home countries, and travel back as often as they can to stay in touch with family and literary life.

In Jayadeva's time, the drama of the young god's courtship of a mortal woman, the woman's yearning for her divine lover, his desertion of her to frolic with other cow-herding girls, their arguments and separation, Radha's pining alone in the forest, Krishna's return to her to plead forgiveness, and finally their joyful union in a leafy glade festooned with flowers, spoke to mortal lovers as well as to spiritual aspirants, as an allegory for all quests, human and divine. Like the *Song of Solomon* for the West, the divine sensuality and "graceful play" of the *Gītāgovinda* inspired succeeding generations of poets and lovers in Bengal and elsewhere in the Subcontinent. The Bengali women poets of today take their inspiration not only from such classic stories, but also from the circumstances of their own lives, to create poems spanning the entire spectrum of "erotic mood and sacred truth."

Carolyne Wright
December
(the Bengali "month of weddings")
2006

Majestic Nights

Love Poems of Bengali Women

First Love   Shamim Azad

In Jamalpur, behind the Public Library,
in the house near the steps down to the river
I first met you.
The sky was filled with fragrance, and
youth, your song

                              was my first love—
Perhaps because you were so young
                    you'd swim away so easily—
before I could turn you into a verse
you eluded me again and again.
All day it was like this—all night, all day
I looked for you through that curtain of smoke.

After a while, profoundly weary, I lay down—
suddenly a sound broke through my sleep:
          even with my eyes closed I could feel
                    the red moonlight outside,
                              the sound of water in the wind,
                                        in the room.
I got up to look for the source, and you
were right next to my heart.

First Sight   Dilara Hashem

Leaf fall at the sinking afternoon's end
The setting woodlands shiver off the beauty of fall
Tyrannical winter's wind
bellows with criminal force

At the National Gallery, an endless line of viewers
for Picasso's early watercolors and oils.
You are among them
and I am viewing you.

You keep pushing your unruly hair
back with your hand, but it keeps falling
ceaselessly forward as if in a child's game.

Your brown eyes keep pulling
my glance away from Picasso's early work
with a magnet's force of attraction—
I'm exhausted by this push and pull.

Tearing myself away I want
to step back but
you come and stand in front of me:
"Can I treat you to a cup of coffee?"
You come and knock upon my wall
of silence—"Please."
My two unruly lips move in spite of me
"Okay."
With this magic touch the entire woodland
                    is covered with flowers.

CW – DH

Dark and Handsome   Taslima Nasrin

When I see you
I want to start my life all over again.
When I see you
I want to die, and dying, turn to holy water.
If you're thirsty sometime, you may touch that water.

I'll give you my sky,
sunlight, rain, whatever you please, just take it.
Embracing your sleeplessness, I'll give you my morphine.

Give me a night twelve years long
in which to see you.
You're more moon than the moon,
in your moonlight I arrange my hair.
Putting vermilion on my forehead someday
                    I'll dress myself up as a woman waiting for her lover.

When I see you
I want to die. If you put fire
in my mouth, I'll die and go to heaven.

CW – MNH

The Other Tongue   Nabaneeta Dev Sen

Come, kiss me,
say you'll never leave me.
Love, take the entire twilight in your hands—
soon darkness will fall,
the path, the landscape, will be blotted out.

Come, kiss me,
then say those words
which only you can utter,
before which not night,
but day and afternoon extend.

Words that have left my lips long ago,
I won't use those leftover sounds
                         to entertain my guest.

Come, kiss me,
then in my veins
I'll echo the fiery silence with that sound,
I'll echo and re-echo the unrevealed sentence.
Let me play in the depths of my ear
the dialogue mingled in the blood.

Come, kiss me,
with your tongue, lips, arteries and veins
let me teach you that language
that's eternally elusive in the ear,
that whispers in the blood.

CW – PB, NDS

Body Theory　　　Taslima Nasrin

This body of mine, known so long,
at times even I can't recognize it.
If a rough hand
with various tricks touches my sandalpaste-smeared hand,
in the house of my nerves a bell chimes,
　　　　　　　a bell chimes.

This my own body,
this body's language I can't read;
it tells its story itself in its own language.
Then fingers, eyes, these lips, these smooth feet,
none of them are mine.
This hand is mine only
yet I don't correctly recognize this hand;
these lips are mine only, these my breasts, buttocks, thighs,
none of these muscles, none of these pores
are under my command, under my control.

In the two-storey house of my nerves
　　　　　　　a bell chimes.
Then in this world whose plaything am I,
man's or Nature's?

In fact not man
but Nature plays me,
I am the sitar of its whims.

At man's touch, I
wake up, breaking out of my slumbering childhood;
in my sea, a sudden high tide begins.

If the sweet scent of love is found in my blood and flesh,
it's Nature only which plays me,
I am the sitar of its whims.

CW – MNH

The Temple   Nabaneeta Dev Sen

For you sky, river, flower, or a book, pictures
For you morning, afternoon, night
For you anything

Far away   among the stars   among your stars
a body of shadows, hard darkness,
a poisoned arrow,
tremors, tremors of earth, tremors of plowed earth,
a vortex of blue agony in an unflinching fist,
(or perhaps the ecstasy of prayer?). Ah,

the most ancient virtue within the first sin.

CW – PB, NS, NDS

Eve Oh Eve   Taslima Nasrin

Why won't Eve eat of the fruit?
Didn't Eve have a hand to reach out with,
fingers with which to make a fist;
didn't Eve have a stomach to feel hunger with,
a tongue to feel thirst,
a heart with which to love?

But then why won't Eve eat of the fruit?

Why would Eve merely suppress her wishes,
regulate her steps?
Subdue her thirst?
Why would Eve be so compelled
to keep Adam moving around in the Garden of Eden
                    all their lives?

Because Eve has eaten of the fruit
                    there are sky and earth,
because she has eaten
                    there are moon, sun, rivers and seas.
Because she has eaten, trees, plants and vines,
because Eve has eaten of the fruit
                    there is joy, because she has eaten there is joy,
joy, joy—
Eating of the fruit, Eve made a heaven of the earth.

Eve, if you get hold of the fruit
                    don't ever refrain from eating.

CW – MNH

Eve Speaks to God　　Kabita Sinha

I was the first
to know
that what rises
is the flip side
of what falls.

As is the light
so is the dark
Your creation
I was the first
to know.

Obeying You
or disobeying
has equal weight
I was the first
to know.

To touch
the tree of knowledge
I was the first
to take
the first bite
of the red apple
I was the first
the first.

I was the first
with the fig leaf
to mark the gap

between shame
and shamelessness
to raise
a wall
between heaven and hell
I was the first.

I was the first
with pleasure's sport
in the body's stem
churning pain
churning tears
I knew how
to fashion
Your image's doll
in laughter in weeping
Your face
in the child's face
I was the first
to see it.

I was the first
to understand
in sorrow in joy
in virtue in sin
our daily lives
no common thing.
I was the first
to break
unalloyed pleasure's
fancy

golden shackle.
I was not Your
dancing puppet
on a string
as was
that scum Adam.

I was the first
insurgent
in Your world
I was the first.

My Dearest
oh my Slave
I was the first
outcaste
banished from paradise
without a home
I knew
that greater than paradise
greater than paradise
was human life
I was the first
to know it.

CW – KS

The Earth Chooses Her Own Husband   Mallika Sengupta

The earth asked, "Who will be my husband?"

The sea replied, "From three sides, I
protect you. I'm the worthy one."

"Not you! I protect myself!
Tell me quick, who's my husband?"

The sun said, "Without me you can't live.
Earth, you're the partner of the sun."

The earth replied, "Throughout the day
I can't endure your scorching heat."

Stars, muses, gods—whoever had
descended from the Milky Way—
their dry love didn't soften Earth.
Then the sky filled with clouds—blue like the blue
of palm trees on the Jamuna's banks.
And the earth raised her eyes at last.

CW – PB

Sunset Colors   "Aparajita Devi" (Radharani Devi)

What do you want? Why have you come today?
. . . You're looking for me? I've got a lot to do.
It's almost time for the Turmeric Shower.
. . . You've got something to say? Maybe later, not now.
Not seeing me, people downstairs may worry,
and come running up here in a flurry.
So—what news of Niraja, by the way?
—She hasn't come here either since that day.
She thinks I'm the guilty one somehow.
Forget all that—why did you come now?
Can you say it fast, what you have to confide?
What's in my hand? Eye makeup for the bride!
I've got no time to be standing here at all—
you've brought back the letters? Ah-h-h, all
those foolish letters All that childish play,
with that you've come running so early in the day?
So that's why you've called at this untimely hour?
I'm astonished at your intellectual power!
If you'd torn them up and thrown them in the trash
we'd have been rid of this nonsense long past.
Instead you've gone to all this fuss
to save them, wrapped in a silk handkerchief, no less!
What's this among the folds? Flower petals, dried.
How strange! They make me want to laugh aloud.

Well then, let's settle this right now!
What should I do with this junk anyhow?
. . . What did you say? I should burn them, at last?
. . . Not keep any tokens from the past?

Right, right, right—your words have great worth!
And I'm the biggest fool on earth!
But I'm still upset by all this stuff!
I wonder when I'll wise up enough!
What did you say? You're asking this of me
for my own good? How senseless can you be?
Step thinking of my good! You know
you gave up that right long ago!
Look after yourself, as you should,
I'll take care of my own good.
. . .Why this pointless cowering, why do you hesitate,
scared for no reason, seems to be your fate!
All right, hold on, let me burn all these
and put an end to your uncertainties.

Well, that was a fine funeral,
not a single trace left at all.
Let's offer this silk kerchief to the fire,
with it I'll feed the letters' pyre.
Wait just a minute, don't go away;
I'll be right back. There's lots more to say.

Here now, these are yours, I've brought them all,
those two pictures taken at Hundru Falls.
You made me sit beside the flowing water
and took my photo yourself, remember?
And here's that journal you wrote in—
such nonsense wrapped in green satin!
Those books of songs and musical notation,
you gave me with so much love and elation.
The year you returned from your Kashmir tour

you gave gift after gift—presents galore.
Embroidered scarves, earrings set with gems,
these saffron flowers, you brought them.
Take all these dried roses, and see
if you can forget their memory.
With your own hand take back this ring.
You slipped it on my finger with so much loving
care and tenderness, when you held my hand
that full-moon night on the Narmada's bank.
You said—no, no, I won't talk this way.
What's the point of all those words today?
Take your things and go back home.
But first I want to ask one question
as I stand on the bank of the River of Death—
is there no society anywhere on earth
where people can forget about caste and color
and become one at heart with each other?
Is there nothing in this world, my dear
that you could cherish more than glamour?
Immense riches, privilege, and honor—
could you find nothing greater?
Disputes, displeasure, sorrow blocking our way,
whatever arrived at our doorway
in poverty's chariot, in condemnation's dust
in all three worlds was what I prized the most.
With your own hand you've insulted it
and sent back the greatest gift of fate.
Alright, let it be! This same nonsense once again!
Let's drop this for all the lives to come!

The *shehnai* is playing in *Raga Ashowari* mode,
the whole house is in a festive mood!
The wedding circle is decked with flowers,
my wedding will be at the twilight hour.
Just look, I've put on so much jewelry,
who else could be so lucky?
In a *Benarasi sari* red as blood,
though Niru still says my fate is sealed
I'll be the queen tonight—she doesn't perceive
That senseless girl is in love with love.
All right—I'm going, farewell then;
know that in this life we'll never meet again.

CW – SMB, NS

Marriage Vessel   Pratima Ray

Her youth spills over as the sun strikes her cheeks
and is reflected back.
Her marriage mark's vermilion smeared from her brow
                 back to the crown of her head.
The mango-leaf veil pulled down to her nose
as if she's some silenced empress.

CW – PB

Love-Timid   Sufia Kamal

Even now the night's intoxication has not passed,
                    eyes filled with passion;
the string of *śiuli*-flowers in the parting of my hair
                    has wilted, the world is overwhelmed with scent.
I have kept the window-shutters open,
                    extinguishing my lamp—
so the dew may enter and cool
                    the fearful outcry of my heart!
Dream's intoxication in my eyes, in my breast
                    a message of hope—
the distant woodland song, birds' twittering
                    will enter here I know.
Rising with a sudden start I see: my heart's monarch,
leaning in silence against my thigh—bedecked with flowers.
He has bestowed heaven on my heated thirst;
my weak and timid heart has trembled,
                    pounding full of love.

CW – AK

Artistry in the Hair   Khaleda Edib Chowdhury

Azure flowers in my hair, fiery mid-day
                    cries out from within—
those arms imbued with amorous delights go stiff,
the tranquil river's flood raises a storm of devotion,
the violin's melody like a love song darkened with words.
Wordlessly I beguile your heart anxious for love—
you will play fanfares if you are mixed up in love
                    on such an afternoon.

Your hands in my hair, on my chin the taste of your tongue—
amorous allure in your lips, your arms artfully arranged,
it seems those clouds you make secretly tremble
                    are watery sunlight's lips
                                or are they wet with dew?

Your eyes on my hair, palms upon my throat
in hot desire, as if with a tremendous noise
                    the whole city stirs.
A river flows in the veins, let the sound
                    of cheerful uproar be heard—
how near to my heart you've come, how near:
I want to preserve those eyes of yours.

                                                CW – AK

35

That Love of Yours Sufia Kamal

I've taken possession of that love of yours
that fills the earth's vessel till it overflows,
filling my eyes, filling my heart,
                    and filling my two hands.
How unbearable is this joy, that this love is so intense.
With the touch, like arrows, of its golden rays
the inner bud blooms, as quickly as grass.
Illumined in my heart, it brings jewel-inlaid riches;
that's why I'm wealthy, my joy will not perish.
With images ever new, this world has gratified me,
given as it is to praise, to perfumed blossoms dripping honey.
The diurnal light of sun, at every watch of the night,
merging hour by hour with your love's every letter, will set.
Ever-new messages I hear;
my heart is overcome—so in love I compose my answering letter.
Warmed from the Sindhu's expanse of river,
                    these clouds upon clouds of gentle moist air
ever bring these love letters, then carry them afar.
The eager heart grows devoted as an unmarried girl,
so it longs to compose scores upon scores
                    of ever-new messages of love and amours.
The heart fills with joy, grows voluble,
                    so I've gathered hence,
from the mortal earth, from the horizon's expanse:
                    impassioned, illumined, that love of yours.

CW – AK

Conjugal Prayer　　　Shamim Azad

How can I live with a saint in perpetual meditation
who renounces everything at night
　　　　　　　　　and goes off to some dream city?
Who in aspect and attire is handsome beyond compare,
for whom a mere woman will not do forever.
A touch to the forehead burns the whole body,
the circle shrinks to the vanishing point.
If, at the Golden Moment, flowers fall in showers,
the sage goes on chanting his vows.
The eyes don't cease blinking at the woman draped in gold,
coals don't glow in the chest.
How could I ever live with a god?
I want a man, not some deity.

At the touch of his fingertips, harvests will flourish;
when the sky clouds over, he'll ask for tea.
The boy who'll take me to see a film by Ray,
to demonstrations, Chinese restaurants, impromptu gossip sessions.
He'll shake down the branches on the bush
　　　　　　　　　to pluck me a scarlet hibiscus,
and if I don't take it, he'll be glum-faced with abashment.
If any day tension should arise between us,
in our travels or in bed he'll regard me as an adversary.
When the last evening's hangover subsides at dawn,
he'll bring me the sky in a deluge.

CW – SMI, SA

37

Which Floor?   Vijaya Mukhopadhyay

The glass cabinet full of crockery grins with its teeth bared.
Some knickknacks called curios fix their gaze on us.
The vulgar white of the walls and the lead-
oxide painted iron grille make faces.

After we moved to a new flat, happiness
threatened to buy us out.
Happiness:
will it come, breaking into this colossal edifice?
All day long, the glass cabinet
shows its teeth.
Unnecessary necessities
scattered all over the place:
clay horses from Bankura, carpets rolled up,
                    books still in their packages.

Happiness that threatened us long ago:
well, we've come home at last.
                         We know now
everyday here we'll be married,
we'll be born in these dark cubicles,
suffer our private deaths, indecisive and ashamed.
Happiness that threatened us, where,
                    which floor?

Grown-Up Boy   Dilara Hafiz

The child spoiled by his parents' excessive pampering,
that ignorant boy hasn't learned the lessons
                    of harsh reality!
His inexperienced lifestyle is a mess—
he's lived so many years but it's as if
                    he hasn't learned how to walk!
In fact he's still a boy—the sun-
                    scorched soil of reality
has never felt the touch of his soft feet!
For this man who's been broken by blows and insults—
I've stretched out my two loving arms,
and with carefree confidence he reached right away
for me! In his eyes I kindle an eagerness for life.

Whatever I can do—I poke at the fire of art,
and in my affections—with all his resolve
the grown-up boy grows up!
As if lover and son were two rooms in one house:
mother and beloved move back and forth between them!
When he returns from the material world
                    smeared with cobwebs and soot,
I rinse him clean in the cool waters of consolation. . .
Day by day, clinging to me,
                    the grown-up boy grows up.

CW – SMI, DH

He Gets Well   Debarati Mitra

You think lack of care
over six years or three days
caused so many pots to break.
You don't know how much I care.
This is a disease of mine,
that everyday I rub even
the golden bowl transparent
with glossy colored polish.
Why then do they go on breaking?
Is the sun so sick with its own radiation
that the spiteful light day after day
                           brings everlasting headaches?

Is it all my fault?
Or does the greedy self-loving Creator
suck the precious nectar only for Himself?
Just as the exhaled breath lights up
the branches of the body, the frustrated lungs,
likewise he gets well
in the giving-over of my life,
my love.

CW – PB

Companion Vijaya Mukhopadhyay

The one with whom we always live
is not called love, but worry.
Love like a visitor
drops in sometimes, with a little smile,
leaves mementoes scattered throughout the house,
then in a flash disappears.

After that, all season long
some of us and worry,
one of us and worry,
we live in the house together
from night to day, day to night.

CW – SBR, VM

The Swaying Lotus   Nabaneeta Dev Sen

If fearless optimism
bespeaks a first-class mind, I
do not have a first-class mind. Hope
blazes from my far-off island, but
oceans and rivers block the way.
Again and again I start out and turn back.
My earthly love —
eternal dew on the swaying lotus of conflict.

Because in late afternoon, after the sun sets
life fades on its own in the mind —
again, because until morning I am secretly
drenched in frightened prayers,
the way therefore isn't straight,
                        but circular. Time and again
after starting out, turning back for home.

In the conflict between the constant and the inconstant
                        indigent, incomprehensible love.

22 May 1960
Bloomington, Indiana

CW – SBR, NS, NDS

Sweaty Canvas   Shamim Azad

Love doesn't linger very long.
At the end of the time it takes, the eyelids
press down heavily over lust-filled eyes.
The song of streaming hair stops
in the monsoon's clammy gusts.
With deep snorts of satisfaction
the hulking buffalo lumbers up
from ditches stinking of fish in June.
Doses of roots and bark won't restore
the long-gone twilight hours of youth.
Even the *Guinness Book of World Records*-
length kiss comes to an end.
The long-faced, laconic, credulous relatives
search for love's telltale signs
when posthumous awards are handed out.

There's no such thing as love in moderation:
it develops with cultivation, concludes in neglect.
Fine art in subjugation won't stay put for long.
Tired breath streams out
of the sweaty canvas,
dejection's doleful shadows
spread through maroon *saris.*
There's no such thing as endless respite
nor can a formula for settled peace be found.
Nobody can be loved for long.

CW – SMI, SA

43

Wife Sanjukta Bandyopadhyay

I keep the southern door closed. In that direction
those who blow their hair through the comb's
                    grinning teeth in the afternoon.
Everyone knows that the three night-faced ones
will call you under their knots of hair. My braided
pattern is not so dark or dense
                    that from this fathomlessness
I can somehow gradually bring it back
                    into the ball of wool.

But I'm in the north.
                    My two needles knitting and purling
will guard both directions.
                    Only from the southern island
does the siren signal danger. And hair blows.

I hold my breath, so that you don't feel
                    this wind or afternoon.

CW – PB

A Child's Babblings   Nabaneeta Dev Sen

As soon as she sees you
that exiled homeless street child
inside my heart, starving the whole day,
starts a tremendous uproar.
Millions of lice bite in her matted hair,
blood bursts from her chapped unoiled skin,
then her shrieks keep all the neighborhood crows away.
Only when she sees you
only when she sees you
that mindless naked child in the depths of my heart
abandons all her games in the dust
and screams out hungrily—"Give, give me love!"
wailing, she stretches out her arms—

Hearing this, her playmates, the street dogs and crows
pause in their snatching games
and keep still for two minutes on the garbage heap.

July-August 1978, Kolkata

CW – PB, NDS

The Blood Mark   Mallika Sengupta

Man, I've never raised my hands against you.

When you first parted my hair to put the blood mark,
that day was I wounded, but I didn't say a word.

On parched earth, no flowers bloom, no peacocks spread their tails,
but we've always dug the sand dunes for your water.
Lifting your sons, we've seen glow-worms, pointed out Orion.

We know the earth's a woman; the sky, first man:
why then have you bound my arms with chains
nor let me see the sky for a thousand years?

Don't insult the earth on which you stand.
Man, I've never raised my hands against you.

CW – PB

Happy Marriage   Taslima Nasrin

My life,
like a sandbar, has been taken over by a monster of a man.
He wanted my body under his control
so that if he wishes he can spit in my face,
                    slap me on the cheek
and pinch my rear.
So that if he wishes he can rob me of my clothes
and take the naked beauty in his grip.
So that if he wishes he can pull out my eyes,
so that if he wishes he can chain my feet,
if he wishes, he can, with no qualms whatsoever,
                    use a whip on me,
if he wishes, he can chop off my hands, my fingers.
If he wishes, he can sprinkle salt in the open wound,
he can throw ground-up black pepper in my eyes.
So that if he wishes he can slash my thigh with a dagger,
so that if he wishes he can string me up and hang me.

He wanted my heart under his control
so that I would love him:
in my lonely house at night,
sleepless, full of anxiety,
clutching at the window grille
                    I would wait for him and sob.
My tears rolling down, I would bake homemade bread,
so that I would drink, as if they were ambrosia,
the filthy liquids of his polygynous body.
So that, loving him, I would melt like wax,
not turning my eyes toward any other man,
I would give proof of my chastity all my life.

So that, loving him
on some moonlit night I would commit suicide
in a fit of ecstasy.

Fire Taslima Nasrin

He is my husband, the dictionary says that he's my
chief, lord, master, et cetera et cetera.
Society agrees that he's my only god.

My doddering old husband has learned well
the prevailing rules and regulations to exert authority.
He's very eager to stroll over the bridge of eternity
                    to the glittering realm of paradise,
he wants all kinds of fruits, brightly-colored cordials and delicious foods,
he lusts after
the fair-skinned bodies of *houris* to chew, suck and lick.

Nothing's written on my forehead but ill fate,
I spend my lifespan in society thrusting chunks of firewood
                    into the oven of these earthly days.
In the afterlife I see my doddering husband
                    exult over the seventy-seven pleasures of sex.

I am alone, in the joyous gardens of paradise I'm alone.
Watching the blind obscenity of men
I burn inside in the everlasting fires of hell,
                    a chaste and virtuous woman.

CW

Divorce Letter   Taslima Nasrin

If you go any distance, you'll no more be mine;
you'll become everybody's playboy.

Going to any body
picking like a vulture at the form and flesh
                    you make your meal.
You perceive no difference between the whore's
                    and the lover's body.

You prefer cunning to poetry.
As night descends, one hundred and one unbridled horses
gallop stampeding through your blood,
the ancestors wake up dancing the rhumba in your blood.
I've told you a lot about moonlight;
you perceive no difference
                    between the new moon and the full.
You prefer affluence to love.
From beneath anybody's heel you lick up
a drop of liquor, you're immersed from head to foot
                    in thousands of gallons of liquor
                              but still your thirst isn't slaked.
I've told you a lot about dreams;
you perceive no difference between the sea and the sewer.
If you go any distance, you'll become everybody's playboy.

He who is everybody's man is never mine.

CW – MNH

Death Beside the Ganga   Sanjukta Bandyopadhyay

Put the mango branch into her hands, with fire
                 and this earth-red silk.

In the heat of this last month of spring, I bend down
                 to touch the Ganga's water.
Its chill creeps up, its round and curving line
runs forward to touch the boat's keel.
I'm taking off my *Shantipuri sari*, bride's iron bangle,
                 all the marks of red.

Water goes on mingling with water, I'll also
                 mingle in that way.
I promise, I'll grow cold inside and out,
                 I'll turn to stone.
Oh Ganga, Ganga, Death has taken the face
                 of my husband's other wife!
Let the conch-shell bangles and the red threads
                 stay around her wrists.

Her shadow comes up today from the water
                 washed with *lac*-dye,
the boat's keel goes on trembling.
Don't tell me again to go back to the body's heat. . .

CW – PB, SB

The Ritual of Satī   Gita Chattopadhyay

The dog has crossed the knee-deep dark stream of water,
that trickle oozing out of your eyes is your Baitarani River.
Your *jāmrul*-tree body covered with poisonous ants,
a hard fist holds you down in case you want to come back.
You're going to burn here, now mount the funeral pyre.
You're going to burn here, now mount the memory pyre.
You're going to burn here—bloody lips, navel the color of copper.
Lift the face-cloth, take a last look at your husband's face.

CW – PB

You, Love   Kabita Sinha

You haven't recognized her, love.
She is your own reflection
but you
didn't turn back to look.

You went away stupid, untrusting,
                    teeth pressed into your lip,
deliberately putting your hands over your eyes
                    to blind yourself;
you didn't show your face.

Do you know, love, on whom you pour disgrace?
Mirrorless, you don't know whose reflection
                    stands before you.
Is she true? Is she constant? Why
                    have you not lifted one finger
to touch her?

Strangely, though, she knows you'll be the one
                    to light the pyre;
she knows, of course, that the last fire always
                    speaks the truth.

Her fate is to go on waiting for your fire.

CW – SMB

What Love is This?   Farida Sarkar

The young man told the Magistrate
that he'd offered her his love,
and when he was refused, he chose
a course of merciless revenge.

What love is this
that drags the beloved out into the street
and pays the homage of ultimate dishonor?
Or with inhuman cruelty
inflicts the most horror-filled
                agonizing death?

If love inspires us to life,
if love's other name is sacrifice,
if it is to live, to create,
then what love is this
which is death and destruction's synonym;
what love is this, where a woman's heart
has no place, only
her body that they seize
                and divide among themselves?

                How many Daisies will die
                before their time, in the murderous
                greedy paws of that so-called love
                before the padlocks on our conscience open?
                And how many Shabmehers
                will have to make their protests known
                alone, alone, at the cost of their lives?

Will the day never come
when all the voices and resolute hands
of every woman and man
obstruct and resist
those ghouls and bloodsuckers?

CW – FS

You Said That the Map Would Be Mine   Nasima Sultana

You said, that house would be mine;
the dark road, yellow house, blue curtains
                in every room, neon lights,
freshly-bloomed roses in flower vases would be mine.
You said, that plot of land, field, farm, water-
                hyacinth pond were mine, all mine;
by the front door a milch cow, a trellis covered
                with bottle gourd,
night-times sleeping under the *śiuli*-tree
                were mine alone.
Why did you say this?

Why did you say my hair would fly
                in the salt-laden wind?
At Worldly Shores on the banks of the rippling river
I'll sit dangling my feet, closed up in my memories,
                and never say a word.

But why have the dark road and yellow house
                not come to be mine?
                        . . . Why not?

But why won't my hair fly in the slippery wind
                of Worldly Shores?
Why won't it fly?
All by itself
my childhood won't play, sinking its face, sinking its hands
                into rice grains filling the granary. . .

Now I'm hungry, now I'm sleepy,
the map in my fist is getting soaked in sweat and blood.
You said that the map would be mine:
why did you say it?

CW – MNH

Disagreement   Ruby Rahman

So I'll get nothing then? I'll have to go away completely empty?
Don't you know that if a beggar is sent off empty-handed like this
the householder comes to grief?—
                    Then why do you turn me away?
My half-acre of land that was drenched in dreams
I mortgaged to you—but still you turn me away!
Tell me how I'll stuff this heavy failure
into my pocket and go off to an arid exile.

So again and again I must return to this sad geography,
leaving behind the dreamless houses and dust-dimmed wayward roads.
There are no fingers soft as earth, no golden
sheaves of rice in the crop-fields.
Asphalt-gray colors call to me with their outstretched hands
and a terrible loss straddles my heart.

I don't know what coins you've put in my hand
                    to send me on my way—
When I asked for the fare—you sneered
                    and dropped a yellow failure on me!
Tell me where shall I find shelter—even my ancestral hearth and home
I've put into your deep palm.
Tell me about any other peasant who's gone away like me,
barren and dispossessed, from such a watery realm of clouds.

Before me lies the golden conflagration of mid-summer;
and I, you see, a landless, trusty ploughman
am left standing here with my futility as long as the three ages.
Even so, will you turn me away?—Can't you take up
rain's liquid plough to till the breast of the soil?

Can't you, when an imperiled moon comes dim-faced
                    to the crop field at the end of night,
create incessant moonlit verses
on the subject of rice-sheaves and the full moon?

CW – SMI, RR

Guiltful　　　Anuradha Mahapatra

You have taken the sky's face.
I take
　　　　the last flower in the giant's garden.
The love-child comes, inspects
my quiet tangle of hair.
My child, or a mistake of nature?
So blooms the flower
of two lowly guiltful lives.

CW – JD

Dismissal Nabaneeta Dev Sen

What can't I do for you? My dear,
whatever is mine is all laid out for you.
Just to see you happy, what can't
I do, my dear!
You said you couldn't stand the smell of *bakul* flowers,
so I chopped down my great-grandfather's *bakul* tree
in the courtyard. Only to see
you happy.
Thinking that jewels might please you,
just look how I've uprooted
my child's heart from my bosom, for
your jewelry box. (Where could I get
any jewel more precious than this!) Just to see
you happy.

But, how strange, my dear, is the play
                    of the human heart!
Even so, you've dismissed me.

9 May 1964
Kolkata

CW – PB, NS, NDS

Love   Dilara Hashem

Whatever wasn't said
let it be put away.

Like *jāmdānī saris* long folded
and left in storage
my heart has given way along the folds.
From the long wait
love turned sour like leftover rice
                    fermented in a water pot,
passion's candle burned down to its end.
Without the fingers' gentle touch
the *tānpurā's* strings got rusted.

How long did you not spread mulch in the garden?
The heart is not a tulip
to bloom on its own in answer to summer.
You thought love is perennial
blooming as usual in disaffection and neglect,
even covered with ice and snow
it will be there, wrapped in the mantle of soil.
That was your mistake.

You thought that like an expensive stereo
decorating the room
love would wait
until you wished to turn it on
and it would play as your heart desired.

But that's not so;
love's not a machine—

telephone and email
can't keep it alive.

You thought everything would stay
as it was before,
that is your mistake.

Love is not ethereal,
it needs organic chemistry.

CW – DH

You (*I*)   Anuradha Mahapatra

You have gone back to her. Seeing Durga's eyes
                 and the constellation of Orion
set together, you've realized the time
                 for the *rāsa*-festival has come.
In the night you're well. . .

        I don't see you anymore. As I
pick up chunks of coal along the roads, I know
you're the life of coal, so inside it

        I set my face on fire in dark fear.

CW – PB

I'll Go Away and I Won't Say a Thing   Nasima Sultana

I'll go away and I won't say a thing.
The way a line of wild ducks, like a boat
hoisting its sail, flies through the air
                and never returns;
the way a couple of counterfeit coins
                fall unnoticed from Mother's drawer,
then after rolling around in the dust
                are finally corroded by mud and soil;
just like that I'll go away and I won't say a thing.

This hand has touched in my childhood's dawn
                the fiercely joyous *tagar*-flower: that memory.
These eyes have seen shame's gooseflesh
                all over the bed: that memory.
This heart quite clearly got neglected: that memory.
This breast sprouted with strident magic: that memory.
All these come no more to mind.
It's only in this wealthy sky, like a shark's fossil
                with no antennae
that there's a frightful rage,
so I'll go away and I won't say a thing.

The way a few courageous people sprint
                toward a moving train;
the way, opening the door in the middle of the night
                a man's libidinous fingers come running in;
like that I'll go away and I won't say a thing.

CW – MNH

What Is There to Fear   Rama Ghosh

If you set me adrift in the sea, in salty water, I go;
if you pull me close, I come, close;
if you make me a slave, I become so.

That star-girl in the sky-lamp will never become
the wild shrub's leaf, the weeds of the marsh.
One day the city dandy came to the country market.
He kissed me and said, "Come to Kolkata.
I'll give you red ribbons, and *saris* edged with gold."
The moment I leaned toward the fathomless depths,
                    he set me adrift with a grin.

If you burn me, too, I'll burn.
Once I'm pulled up by the roots
                    what is there to fear!

CW – PB

Friend   Anuradha Mahapatra

No friends remain, only indifferent people—
            The one who said this is not
an unknown dark thinker. He lives in the city
            with his wife and daughter,
goes up the darkened spiral staircase
            to the roof terrace trembling with earthquakes,
remembers the crescent-moon building
            not far away, remembers ages ago,
from out of the Ganga, from the goddess's order,
            his life in marriage
had started happily; this feeling tears him apart.
Between the male and female stork of the village
            images of rivers and hunting remain.
I look at him; from the separation of the female stork
            I pull his Ganga-deep
wish to the swaying stage
            where death and life are equal.

CW – PB

The Empress's Love   Mallika Sengupta

Have I kissed more than the countless stars in the sky
of my kingdom? Whose loving face rests now on my knees?

Whose innocent dragonfly-blue eyes? Conquering
the world, boys of this land brought laurels and prestige,

a death-warrant for the ruling lady's heart.
Why do you look at me like that in a crowd,

enchanting stag? Have you no young beloved?
I, at fifty, the leftover dross of gold.

Come down the chasm's steps, let the kingdom's
politics leave me, its sense of public shame.

But if they raise their hands to say that shame
danced in my blood with its peacock tail fanned,

if the chain of command shatters, if scandal starts
to turn men's thoughts, why look at me like that,

enchanting stag? My life is gone, my beauty
wreaked only havoc, body left gaunt with the fears
of earth, ants finishing off the honey of love.

CW – PB

When There Was Land   Ketaki Kushari Dyson

When there was land
and you weren't hard to find,
I could walk to your threshold in a cloud of dust.

A time came
when there was land
but your house was empty.
Then the dust was my road,
what sustained me on the road,
and my road's end as well.

Now there's no land,
nor are you anywhere;
flood waters stretch to the horizon's coconut trees.

I push and push my pole
and make my way through the waters
in the din of a thousand boats,

hoping that by chance
my planks may strike your planks.

Now there's only one line that's open,
the seamless line of water.

Light grows dim.
Water gets on my boards.
The few landmarks,
the round half-sunk heads
of trees and houses,
fade from my eyes.

Night's navigation is unknown to me,
and all around me they shout: take care,
take care.

Come back as landing steps.

You're In My Core   Shahera Khatun Bela

The blooming rose of time has sobbed,
as if here the flower-dialogue were robbed!
I've never been happy in this world;
still, let roses bloom throughout the world.

The monsoon months pour down in this meadow,
                    in this wood;
still, memories will never recede.
I know there's no all-triumphant domain.
You're in my core, call me by any name.

CW – MNH

Love is Solitude   Rajlakshmi Devi

Don't you know that love is only solitude?
A single star inserted in the far-flung sky.
This rope suspended from one shore to the other,
From the twilight of lovelessness to love's prodigious dark.
If the mansion is unliveable, the forest's a disaster.
At the end of a separation seven ages long,
                    the chant of eternal solitude.
Let existence's domain lie in sleep's thrall;
Love, sleepless sentry, will raise its midnight call.
The storm-bedraggled crow will shake its wings over the beloved's yard;
                    This, too, is a sign of love. But this the final word:
                    Love is just humanity—a kind of poverty.
                    A transcendence from one aloneness to another.

CW – SMB

This Afternoon Knows   Ruby Rahman

Someone has left some vapor in my heart,
art's ritual water—deep as midnight.
Someone has left a hidden wonder,
left a spellbinding moonrise—
Today they all hover above my heart like late spring leaves—
this afternoon in which they play the listless finger cymbals,
this afternoon oblique and indolent
as the final month of autumn, reclining from the tops of trees,
leaning over the still green water of a hyacinth pond,
and on the unsoaked wings of a duck diving under tangled water vines.
Unmoved afternoon goes on hanging from the eaves
of distant houses, immobile and immense.

But this afternoon knows that someone is coming,
someone traveling a vast distance,
bringing someday in his cold hard hand
something that nobody could ever give.

Before giving birth to a child, a woman knows
when the moment is upon her: the advent of man.
This afternoon knows—
how I tremble with this advent at this late hour!

Perhaps he's come ever so much closer,
on my back the deep warmth of his breath.
Perhaps the time of his arrival has not yet come—:
as I sink into sleep some nights
his hairy hard cold hand touches my breast.

This afternoon-time, unworried in the dull-faced sun
reaches me from afar with his long cold hand
and suddenly grabs my own worn, grubby hand.
Could I have known this as my auspicious moment?
But this afternoon knows—
this afternoon knows everything.

CW – SMI, MNH, RR

Hope   Rajlakshmi Devi

"Do you write poetry or sing?
Believe me, I knew nothing about it."
I never hoped that you would come.
At the crossroads of fate I'd stopped alone
And promised that whichever guest would come,
I'd give him everything, body, mind, and soul.
I never hoped for anyone handsome.

I never hoped you would be talented.
I knew for certain—I'd embellish you
With talent—from the riches of my heart.
And you'd grow magnificent in the brilliance of my service.
Your pride of life would make you
Supreme. With my primordial trust in this unchanging truth,
I never hoped you'd have any virtue.

I never hoped you'd love me.
As though, if I leaped, I'd find a foothold
Even at the bottom of the sea.
As if, left to drift in the current,
The boat would find its way to shore.
To my highest question—that worthy inquiry,
I never hoped to find an answer.

CW – MM

This Blunder Wrapped in Silk   Shahera Khatun Bela

This I burned in the conflagration of your might
and you became my lord in a moment's delight.
Sometimes in your somber face
                    the fountain's water flows by,
sometimes only sinless blood rolls down the sky.
Can I blossom, an obstinate flower
                    in grape's milk?
That I did not receive you earlier—
                    a blunder wrapped in silk.

Mira's Hymn   Dilara Hafiz

Like a lame beggar I
have stretched out my hands towards you;
you keep holding on with both hands
                     to an empty cup. See
if I haven't reached out with both my hands
again and again towards even greater emptiness?

With a lame beggar's expectation
I've stretched out my hands only towards you—
as if in exchange for a nickel maybe
or a dime! — To you I can give
the golden key to the mansion of dreams
hidden very close to my heart.

Like a lame beggar I've gone on
stretching out my hands in your direction—
Motionless as matter, I am that blind beggar
when I can't make out any features
in the abyss of night! Still then I
keep my hands stretched out towards you
in silent dedication.

Your songs of praise, your hymns
suffused through my body, fill my whole being:
I've kept my hands stretched out
only towards you, a golden conflagration in my heart—
a thirsty craving heat in my lips,
I've kept an unquenchable fire burning—
Waiting for you, I've kept a midnight vigil
and heard the distant resonance of the *sarod*:

a pure memento—why does this distress,
these wounded feelings, pull me toward sorrow's tryst?
Who knows how far away and where the distance is—
the virgin days and nights
                              are indolent, unstrummed!
Who knows when, how long ago you hoisted
over my *sampan* your victory flag. . . .

You're still immersed in the depths of wine;
haven't you quenched your thirst? — Now come,
finish your bathing in my gentle spirits—
I've captured Mira's ardor in my being.
Like a blind beggar ceaselessly
I've kept on stretching out,
stretching out my hands.

CW – SMI

Rice Sheaves This Alluvial Night   Khaleda Edib Chowdhury

With what cruel desire the dispassionate night stays wide awake—words of lamentation covering their faces with the pure white scarves of mist and moving on—receiving intermittent flashes at the touch of hydro-electric power. I don't know whether satisfaction comes or not, nor can I tell if its long sigh on the wind can be heard; even still it seems to come, gliding along the earth. In the water's depths I see the blue of the sky. Standing in the deep night's channel, I think—"Oh night, you've come, it seems, from some unknown land of moonlight."

Like the sound of rain, moonlight drips down. In the mist, a sleepy feeling descends upon the eyelids. But sleep doesn't come—the blood runs wild with untamed desire, yet how cruel this longing is! What a furious burning in my body! Ah love, you tell me, is this God's great universe? A night of gilded dreams bewildered by the scent of flowers? What restlessness is this! In the blood's channel the dazzling summons of an irresistible will, it seems love's gold chariot is moving at the speed of a ruined wind.

I know, night comes like this, like this the hard-won moment comes. I pronounce my life's longings with a touch of wondrous affection. In midnight's musical soiree, tender yet peculiar glances are exchanged. The celestial nymph descends with the night's light in her hand.

This is how the night of enchantment stays awake—yet still dispassionate—as if the murmuring flowers of love bloomed helplessly. The body's desires grow like plants. Such a night—ah, that is a wealth of longing. A night without mourning or prayers, murmuring in consciousness acceptable to the sight, turns a woman into a surging river—her lover composes in her body a starwheel of dreams. The unparalleled desires of the man thirsting to travel go on throbbing in tones of the sacred river's song. Ah! what a conspiracy of treasure in the blood! In the endless deep darkness—in the stream of naked pleasure, the sporting ground is moved by a melancholy mystery. Is this the promise of life?

Immersed for thousands of years in the depths of creation, man inwardly nourishes his wisdom and consciousness in the tree of nature and desire. In the middle of the silent yet ever-lengthening night, a gloomy sense of sorrow gnaws away at this starving soul. What a heartless, bitter form of life! In the darkness of such a night, what impenetrable unhappiness!

But still this night must be understood once more. A man must know the object of his longing. Just as unending time goes on all over the world, so the lover in that stream of time cuts love's treasure-laden body into pieces with the dagger of his will—all night, thousands of torches will go on burning, red and blue lamps, thirsty lips will be crushed by blossoming kisses. The seeds of love will be sown throughout the land, like the blessing of God.

CW – AK, AUMF

The Majestic Night   Dilara Hafiz

The majestic night, the dark of night,
The thirst-allaying moonlight.
In the forest of long grass, white flowers bloom.
Radha is sitting in wait, alone
In her happiness divine. . . .
The love story of all time
The poet writes in the Middle Ages,
In poetry he paints her images.

Stealthily breaking the pot of curd
Dark Krishna crossed the River of the Dead,
But in dark clouds compassionate
She finds eternal happiness at Krishna's feet.

Across thousands of years
Within their hearts they're together. . . .
Still, in her happiness, sorrow's thorn
Brings ebb-tide to the River of Time.

CW – SMI

Notes on the Poems

Dark and Handsome (Taslima Nasrin)

Married Bengali Hindu women put vermilion paste in the parting of their hair; Muslim Bengali women do not use such a sign of marriage. In times of tension between Muslims and members of the minority Hindu community in Bangladesh, Bangladeshi Hindu women refrain from wearing vermilion.

In the Hindu cremation ceremony, the funeral pyre is customarily lit by the closest male relative. If a wife dies and there is no son, the husband may perform the rite. The fire is applied first to the mouth of the deceased.

All Bengalis, Hindu or Muslim, understand the imagery of the Hindu rites of marriage and death. In literature, this imagery has high recognition value, even among Muslims, so Bengali Muslim writers tend to employ a great deal of imagery from Hindu lore and customs.

Body Theory (Taslima Nasrin)

The Bengali for "body theory" is *dehatattwa*, a Sanskrit-derived term which can also mean "anatomy" or "physiology," although most physicians simply use the English medical terms. The more immediate associations of *dehatattwa* for a Bengali reader would be the Tantric doctrine that the body is the seat of all knowledge, and its esoteric implication that sexual acts can thus be employed as spiritual exercises in the search for union with the Divine.

Eve Oh Eve (Taslima Nasrin)

The story of Adam's and Eve's eating of the fruit of the Tree of Life, and being expelled from the Garden of Paradise, is found in several passages in the Koran.

The Earth Chooses Her Own Husband (Mallika Sengupta)

The Jamuna is a river of North India, flowing past Delhi and Agra.

Sunset Colors ("Aparajita Devi"; Radharani Devi

The Turmeric Shower (*holudmākhan*) is a ceremony taking place before the Bengali Hindu wedding, in which the bride, wearing a yellow or ochre-colored *sari*, is anointed with turmeric paste by female friends and family members of the wedding party. Water mixed with this paste is sent to the groom's party for his own turmeric ceremony as a symbol for how the couple's bodies and destinies will soon be mingled.

The *shehnai* is a reed instrument, similar to an oboe in shape and timbe, traditionally played at Bengali weddings.

Raga Ashowari is a classical North Indian *rāgā*, similar in structure to the Aeolian mode in ancient Greek music. As a *rāgā* traditionally played in the morning, it conveys the time of day in which this meeting between former lovers is occuring.

The *Benarasi* is a costly silk *sari*, richly embroidered with gold threads, traditionally made by families of weavers of Benares (Varanasi). Red ones are worn as wedding *saris* by Bengali brides from affluent families.

MARRIAGE VESSEL (Pratima Ray)

The marriage vessel (*ghat* in Bengali) is a small pot placed between the bride and groom during the Hindu wedding ceremony. It is inscribed with a totemic human figure—both guardian and fertility emblem—and filled with mango leaves that droop down over the pot's rim. The human figure is painted with the same vermilion paste with which the groom marks the parting of his bride's hair toward the end of the ceremony. (This mark is much thicker and heavier for the new bride.) The analogy between *ghat* and bride—both of them marriage vessels—should be clear.

LOVE-TIMID (Sufia Kamal)

Siuli, the night jasmine, is a small, sweet-scented flower which blooms at night in the months after the monsoon (September to November). It is often used to make garlands and decorations for the parting of the hair of the Bengali Muslim bride.

CONJUGAL PRAYER (Shamim Azad)

The "dream city" is Alaka, the legendary capital of King Kubera, popularly regarded in Hindu lore as the lord of wealth.

Satyajit Ray of Kolkata (1921-1992) was India's most renowned film director. His films are now world-famous, and it is quite fashionable among Bengali intellectuals and educated young people to attend them. The actual film named in the poem is *Charulatā*.

WHICH FLOOR? (Vijaya Mukhopadhyay)

The words in Bengali for "colossal edifice" are *bisāl yajñsālā* (literally, immense hall of ritual sacrifice), referring to a hall or building for Vedic animal sacrifices or ancient religious rituals. The term also suggests a site of hectic, even meaningless activity.

The poet herself has lived for many years in a flat in one of the first modern high-rise apartment buildings constructed in South Kolkata.

Bankura is a village in the hill country of West Bengal known for its stylized figurines of horses fashioned from the local red clay. Traditional offerings of poor villagers at rural Hindu temples and Islamic shrines, these figurines have become popular tourist items and decorations in the homes of upper middle-class Bengali intellectuals.

THE SWAYING LOTUS (Nabaneeta Dev Sen)

The word *dhruba*, translated here as "constant," is also the Bengali name for the Pole Star, and for a prince known for his unwavering devotion to Hari (one aspect of Krishna).

THE BLOOD MARK (Mallika Sengupta)

The "blood mark" refers to the vermilion paste with which the groom marks the parting of his bride's hair during the Hindu marriage ceremony.

After the Moghul invasion of India, upper-class Hindu women (who did not have to work outside, in the fields) began to be secluded in *purdah*, like their Muslim sisters, supposedly to protect them from attacks by Muslim males. After marriage, therefore, the virtuous Hindu woman was not supposed to look upon any man except her husband: this prohibition extended to the male gods of the Vedic pantheon, including the sky!

HAPPY MARRIAGE (Taslima Nasrin)

In the estuaries of the great rivers emptying into the Bay of Bengal, new shoals and sandbars are continually being formed from the tons of silt washed downstream every year. In overpopulated Bangladesh, these formations are zealously watched. As soon as they rise even a fraction above the normal tide line, they are settled and cultivated. The first to take possession is the owner. It was from such exposed and fragile islands that an estimated 139,000 people were washed away in the devastating cyclone and tidal bore of April 1991.

FIRE (Taslima Nasrin)

The *houris* are the celestial virgins promised to all faithful Muslims—male Muslims, that is—as consorts in paradise. There are no equivalent male consorts promised to faithful Muslim women.

DEATH BESIDE THE GANGA (Sanjukta Bandyopadhyay)

According to Hindu tradition, the person who can be brought to the side of the holy river Ganga (Ganges) to die will bypass the round of births or deaths remaining to her, and go straight to salvation. All the items named in the poem (*Shantipuri sari*, iron bangle, red threads around the wrist, conch-shell bangle, and *lac*-dye to outline the soles of the feet), as well as the color red in general, are signs of marriage for the Hindu woman. It is customary for a deceased woman to be dressed in her bridal finery before being brought to the funeral pyre for cremation.

THE RITUAL OF SATĪ (Gita Chattopadhyay)

On September 4, 1987, in the village of Deorala in Rajasthan, an eighteen-year-old Rajput woman, Roop Kanwar, burned herself alive on the funeral pyre of her husband, setting off storms of controversy, and a flurry of legislation, in the country. Alleged eyewitnesses first claimed that the girl committed *sati* voluntarily, this being a long-revered custom for Rajput widows.

Later, however, after the central and state governments voiced tardy disapproval, and sent police to close off the area to thousands of fervent pilgrims and curiosity seekers, the story emerged that the young woman had been dragged to the pyre, screaming for mercy, by her in-laws who were anxious for the glory—and revenue—that accrue to Rajasthani villages where a *sati* has occurred. Although the custom was outlawed in 1829, it remains very much alive in cultural memory; but fortunately, despite the intense publicity this incident received, there have been no substantiated "copy-cat" cases.

Jāmrul wood is often used for funeral pyre fuel.

In Hindu mythology, the Baitarani (*Baitarani*) is the river that the spirits of the dead must cross to reach the afterworld, much like the Styx or the Jordan in Western mythology.

You, Love (Kabita Sinha)

According to Hindu custom, the funeral pyre is always lit by the closest male relative of the deceased—usually the eldest son. If a wife dies and there is no son, the husband may perform the rite. Generally, the one who lights the pyre is also supposed to be the heir.

What Love is This (Farida Sarkar)

Lutfun Nahar Daisy was a fourteen-year-old honors student from Kaliganj village in Bangladesh, who was the object of the obsessive attentions of a young man, Mahmudur Rahman Hasan, of the same village. Despite the girl's own youth and lack of interest, as well as her parents' ordering Hasan to leave Daisy alone, he felt insulted and decided to take revenge.

On the night of January 14, 1990, Hasan and a group of accomplices attempted to abduct Daisy as she went out of her house to the latrine. When she resisted, they poured kerosene on her and set her on fire. She died six days later in the burn unit of Dhaka Medical College Hospital, amidst great public outrage. The young man and his accomplices were arrested soon after the murder, and brought to trial in May 1990.

Shabmeher was another young Bangladeshi girl from a poor village who was lured into prostitution when a family acquaintance promised her mother that he would arrange a good job for her. The man took Shabmeher to Tanbazar, a town in the Narayanganj district near Dhaka, notorious for its brothels and other criminal activities. When the horrified girl realized what her "job" was to be, she protested and refused to cooperate. The procurer and his henchmen gang-raped her and beat her to death. Shabmeher's story was dramatized in a short film produced by Dhaka University in 1989.

Love (Dilara Hashem)

Jāmdānī saris are among the most costly of all *saris* produced in East Bengal. They are woven of fine muslin with embroidered designs—flowers, birds, and geometrical patterns—and are highly prized. But if they remain folded and unused for a long time, the fabric tends to weaken and split along the creases, so women try to refold them frequently.

The rice in the second stanza is *pāntā*, which refers to the custom in villages without refrigeration of storing leftover cooked rice in cool water in earthen pots, where it can ferment and go sour.

You (I) (Anuradha Mahapatra)

The *rāsa*-festival celebrates the *rāsa-līlā*, or dancing of Krishna with Radha and the *gopīs*. The festival takes place on the full moon of the Bengali month of Kartik (mid-October to mid-November), not long after the ten-day celebration of Durga Puja in late September or early October.

WHAT IS THERE TO FEAR (Rama Ghosh)

Many residents of Kolkata used to hang what they called a "sky-lamp" from the lightning rod on the roof of their houses. The light shining out of the metal lamp frame had a girl's form, and came to be called the *tārāmeye* ("star-girl").

MIRA'S HYMM (Dilara Hafiz)

Mirabai was a Rajput princess of the 16th century, who became a fervent devotee of the Lord Krishna and composed hundreds of *bhajan*—hymns of praise—to him, many of which are still performed by Indian classical singers today.

The "unquenchable fire" of stanza four is *raban-citā* in Bengali, the eternal fire in which the demon Ravana, anti-hero of the epic *Rāmāyana*, burns after his death in battle against the hero Rama.

THE MAJESTIC NIGHT (Dilara Hafiz)

The story of the love between the cowherd girl Radha and the god Krishna is one of the most popular subjects of medieval Bengali Vaisnava poems and songs, especially the *Gītāgovinda* of Jayadeva, Bengal's renowned Sanskrit poet. Even in predominantly Muslim Bangladesh, these lyrics and the Hindu traditions from which they emerge have a great effect on literature and culture, and such references to Hindu mythology are frequent in the work of Bangladeshi Muslim poets and writers.

Radha ("sitting in wait, alone") is often portrayed as dwelling in *birahālay*, the state of separation from and pining for her lover, the dark-skinned Krishna, especially after his work on this earth is finished and he crosses the river Baitarani, the Hindu equivalent of the Styx, the River of the Dead.

About the Poets

Shamim Azad, born in 1954 in Jamalpur, Mymensingh district, East Bengal, attended Dhaka University during the 1971 War of Liberation for Bangladesh, and ultimately received her B.A. and M.A. with Honours in Bengali Literature from Dhaka University. After her marriage, she worked as a journalist and college lecturer in Dhaka, and in 1990 moved with her family to England to teach Bangladeshi immigrant children for the Inner London Educational Authority. She writes poetry, fiction, and drama, and is active in the South Asian literary community in the U. K.

Sanjukta Bandyopadhyay, born in 1958 in Howrah, near Kolkata, received a B.A. with Honours from Presidency College/University of Kolkata; and a M.A. in Comparative Literature and a degree in Library Science from Jadavpur University. She works as a librarian for Howrah Bally Girls' School, and lives with her husband and family in South Kolkata. She has published several books of poetry.

Shahera Khatun Bela, born in 1956 in Dhaka, received her medical degrees from Sir Salimullah Medical College/Dhaka University, specializing in Anesthesiology. She teaches in the Department of Anesthesiology at Dhaka's Institute of Postgraduate Medicine and Research, and practices medicine at the affiliated Postgraduate (P. G.) Hospital. She lives with her physician husband and family in central Dhaka, and has published several collections of poetry.

Rajlakshmi Devi Bhattacharya, born in 1927 in Mymensingh (now in Bangladesh), received degrees with Honours from Calcutta University, and has lived in Patna, Pune, and Addis Ababa, Ethiopia, where her physicist husband held professorships. She received her Ph.D. and taught Philosophy as Department Chair at Pune University until retirement, writing many volumes of poetry, fiction, and memoir, and translating some of her poetry to English. She lives in Pune with her husband.

Gita Chattopadhyay, born in 1941 into a traditional landholding family in North Kolkata, was educated at Lady Brabourne College/University of Calcutta. She has devoted herself to writing—mainly of poetry and literary criticism—and to extensive reading in Bengali, Sanskrit, and English. Although she has given readings for All-India Radio, she lives essentially in seclusion, and remains an elusive and highly respected figure in contemporary Bengali letters. Since the deaths of her parents, she has lived with a brother and two sisters, all unmarried, in the family's 175-year-old ancestral home, now surrounded by one of Kolkata's busiest commercial districts next to the Sealdah Railway Station.

Khaleda Edib Chowdhury, born in 1939 in Kumilla, East Bengal, received degrees in Education and Bengali Literature from Dhaka University, then entered government service where she has worked as a publication officer. She lives with her family in Uttarpara, Dhaka, where she writes and has published several volumes of poetry as well as over a dozen books for children.

Radharani Devi (1904-1989), a beloved Kolkata literary figure, published in the 1930s her most famous work—a series of poems, in the voices of women, in traditional form but groundbreaking colloquial diction—under the pseudonym "Aparajita Devi." Married and widowed at a young age, she corresponded from *purdah* (seclusion) with the eminent Kolkata writer Narendra Dev, and eventually the two writers married, at a time when remarriage for a Hindu widow of good family was very rare. The couple had one daughter, Nabaneeta. Their house in south Kolkata was a famous meeting place for poets and writers; she lived there with her daughter and granddaughters until the end of her days.

Nabaneeta Dev Sen, born in 1938 in Kolkata, daughter of renowned Bengali poets Radharani Devi and Narendra Dev, and first wife of Nobel Prize-winning economist Amartya Sen, received degrees in English and Comparative Literature at Presidency College/University of Calcutta; Jadavpur University; Harvard University (M.A.), and Indiana University

(Ph.D.). Professor Emerita of Literature at Jadavpur University, she is one of the most popular and prolific writers of her generation, having published over two dozen volumes of poetry, fiction, memoir, and literary criticism. With her mother, Radharani Devi, she co-edited the prize-winning *The Collected Aparajita Poems*, and she travels world-wide for readings, conferences, and visits to her daughters in Delhi and New York.

Ketaki Kushari Dyson, born in 1940 in Kolkata, received degrees with highest Honours from Presidency College/University of Calcutta, and her Ph.D. in English Literature from Oxford University. Based in England since her marriage, she stays in close contact with Bengali literary life, and travels to Kolkata frequently to visit family and participate in literary conferences and festivals. She has published some two dozen volumes of poetry, fiction, drama, essays, and research-based scholarly works in both Bengali and English. She is also a noted and versatile literary translator, rendering Anglo-Saxon poetry into alliterative Bengali and the poetry of Rabindranath Tagore and other noted Bengali authors into English.

Rama Ghosh, born in 1944 in Srirampur near Kolkata, received degrees with Honours in Sanskrit and Education from Serampore College/Burdwan University and Calcutta University, and teaches Sanskrit and Literature at a girls' college preparatory high school in Saradapalli, a village near Srirampur, where she lives with her family. She has published several books of poetry.

Dilara Hafiz, born in 1955 in Garpara, Manikganj district, East Bengal, received her degrees in Bengali Literature and in Education from Dhaka University, and lives with her husband, noted Bangladeshi poet Rafiq Azad, and their two sons in Dhaka, where their home is a major meeting place for poets and writers from all over Bangladesh and West Bengal. She teaches at Eden Girls' College in Dhaka and has published several books of poetry.

Dilara Hashem, born in 1936 in Jashor (Jessore) near Kolkata in Bengal, moved with her family to Dhaka after the 1947 Partition of India sent many Bengali Muslims to East Pakistan. After her marriage, she moved with her family to Karachi, West Pakistan, where she worked as a singer and radio announcer and producer. After a few years in the new nation of Bangladesh, she moved with her family to the U.K. and then the U.S., where she lives in northern Virginia, works for Voice of America's Bangla Service, and has published some two dozen volumes of fiction and poetry, as well as film and television film scripts. A very popular novelist in Bangladesh, she travels frequently to Dhaka to visit family and maintain contact with Bengali literary life.

Begum Sufia Kamal (1911-1999), born in *purdah* into an aristocratic land-holding family in Barisal, East Bengal, was Bangladesh's most revered poet, hero of the Bangladesh liberation movement, and advocate of human rights and women's education and opportunities. She lived in Kolkata during her first marriage, taught in a Muslim girl's school after she was widowed, met and was inspired by Mahatma Gandhi and other social and political reformers, and moved to Dhaka with her second husband and family in 1947 after the Partition of India and Pakistan. During the Bangladesh Liberation War of 1971, when the Bengalis of East Pakistan fought for independence, Sufia Kamal and her family worked in the resistance, treating wounded fighters and helping their families and other victims of the war. One of her own teenaged sons working for the resistance was killed during this period. After Bangladesh gained its independence, Sufia Kamal was recognized as one of the new nation's leading literary figures, and honored as the spiritual "First Lady" of the Bangladeshi people. She published some two dozen books of poetry and prose in her lifetime, including a diary-memoir of the Liberation War, and she was active in women's social service organizations, an inspiration for younger generations of Bengalis. After her death in late 1999 in Dhaka, she was buried with full state honors, the first woman in Bangladesh to be so recognized.

Anuradha Mahapatra, born in 1957 into a working-class family in Nandigram village in the Medinipur district of rural West Bengal, attended college in Nandigram and then received an M.A. in Bengali Literature from Calcutta University, the first woman in her family to pursue higher education. Living and working in Kolkata for social service organizations and as a community educator for slum children, she has published several books of some of the most original poetry being written today in Bengali, and has traveled to Europe and the U.S. to read her work at conferences and festivals. A volume of translations of her work by Carolyne Wright and co-translators Jyotirmoy Datta and Paramita Banerjee, *Another Spring, Darkness: Selected Poems of Anuradha Mahapatra*, was published by Calyx Books in 1996, to wide acclaim.

Debarati Mitra, born in 1946 in Kolkata, received a B.A. from Ashutosh College of Calcutta University, and an M.A. from Jadavpur University, both in Bengali Literature. Since her marriage, she has lived in South Kolkata with her family and devoted herself to writing and publishing several volumes of poetry and literary criticism.

Vijaya Mukhopadhyay, born in 1937 in Dhaka, came to Kolkata to study Sanskrit, Bengali and English, and received B.A. and M.A. with Honours from Presidency and Sanskrit Colleges of Calcutta University, and more recently her Ph.D. in Sanskrit Dramatics from Calcutta University. She teaches Sanskrit at Ramakrishna Sarada College, translates, edits and writes for several publications, and has published several acclaimed volumes of poetry. She lives in south Kolkata with her husband, poet Sarat Kumar Mukhopadhyay, and reads and lectures widely.

Taslima Nasrin, born in 1962 in Mymensingh, East Bengal, trained as a medical doctor and worked for several years at Dhaka hospitals and clinics. She made her reputation as a poet and social commentator in Dhaka, and then won a major Kolkata literary award in 1992 for a collection of her op-ed columns and essays that criticized political leaders, literary figures, and conservative religious values that conspired to oppress women.

Her short novel, *Lajja* (Shame), angered conservative Bangladeshi Muslim clerics, who called for her death and helped make her situation an international *cause celebre*. She was smuggled out of Bangladesh in 1994 and has lived mainly in Europe and the U.S. ever since, writing, publishing, and speaking worldwide. On several recent visits to Kolkata, Nasrin has sought to attain Indian citizenship and residency rights, so far unsuccessfully. A volume of translations of her poetry by Carolyne Wright and co-translators, *The Game in Reverse: Poems by Taslima Nasrin* (George Braziller, 1995), was the very first work of hers available in English. Poems from this collection been been reprinted widely in anthologies and on the internet, often without permission from or credit to the translators.

Ruby Rahman, born in 1946 in Dhaka, received her B.A. and M.A. degrees with Honours in Bengali, English, and Psychology from Dhaka University, and teaches English at a commercial college in Dhaka. She has served on the Bangladesh national review board for textbooks and educational curricula, organized national poetry festivals, and produced and appeared in literary programs on radio and television while raising her family and traveling with her husband, a labor leader and politician. She is among the most highly regarded poets active in Bangladesh today.

Pratima Ray, born in 1942 in Kolkata, graduated from St. Margaret's School, worked for several years, and since her marriage has lived in South Kolkata with her family, publishing poetry in leading magazines and in several individual collections and anthologies.

Farida Sarkar (1957-2005) was born in Rajshahi, East Bengal, received her B.A. and M.A. with Honours in English at Dhaka University, taught at colleges in Dhaka, and worked as an announcer for Radio Bangladesh and as a government administrator. In 1991, she received a Fulbright Fellowship to the United States, and after completing a Ph.D. in English at SUNY Stony Brook, she worked for Voice of America Bangla Service before returning to Dhaka. She published volumes of poetry and worked with Carolyne Wright to translate other Bangladeshi women poets. After a lengthy struggle with cancer, she died in March 2005 in Dhaka.

Mallika Sengupta, born in 1960 in Kolkata, grew up in small towns in West Bengal where her father was posted as a government officer. She received degrees in Sociology from Calcutta University, teaches Sociology at Maharani Kasiswari College, Kolkata, and contributes actively to Kolkata literary magazines and literary festivals. She has published several books of poetry, some in collaboration with her husband, poet Subodh Sarkar.

Kabita Sinha (1931-1998) was born in Kolkata into a traditional landowning family of the Kshatriya caste, educated at home and at the University of Calcutta in English and Bengali Literature. She married writer and publisher Bimal RayChoudhury (a Brahmin) in spite of opposition from both families to inter-caste marriage, and worked for the Indian Government, particularly All India Radio, most of her life, as a correspondent, producer, and station director. For her more than fifty books—novels, short story collections, and volumes of poetry—she received major awards, including a residency fellowship at the International Writing Program at the University of Iowa. After retirement, she divided her time between Kolkata and the Boston home of her younger daughter, where she died after a sudden illness, one day before her 67th birthday.

Nasima Sultana (1957-1997) was born in Kushtia, a town near the border with West Bengal, daughter of Murshidabadi Muslim refugees who came to East Pakistan after the 1947 Partition of India. After receiving her B.A. and M.A. with Honours in English from Rajshahi University, she came to Dhaka to work as a journalist for newspapers and magazines, and married a fellow journalist, Ahsan Hakim Tutul. She wrote and published poetry and short fiction as one of Bangladesh's most promising younger writers until her tragic death in November 1997 after a short battle with cancer.

About the Translators

Paramita Banerjee, born in 1958 in Kolkata, received a B.A. with Honours in Philosophy from Presidency College/University of Calcutta, and has completed her Ph.D. in Social Philosophy on a research fellowship from Jadavpur University. She was active in student politics as an undergraduate, writes for theatre and literary magazines, and has translated several Bengali novels into English for Penguin India. With Carolyne Wright, she prepared initial English versions of poems by many of the leading West Bengali women poets represented here. She works for non-governmental organizations to provide social services and education to the children of prostitutes and other residents of the urban slums. She lives with her family in south Kolkata.

Swapna Mitra Banerjee, born in 1964 in Kolkata, received a B.A. with Honours at Presidency College, and an M.A. from the University of Calcutta, both in history. She joined her husband, a physicist, in the U.S., completed her Ph.D. in history at Temple University, and has taught at Brown and at the University of Florida, where she has recently received tenure. She worked with Carolyne Wright in Kolkata and later in Philadelphia on translations of a few Bengali women's poems.

Jyotirmoy Datta, born in 1936 in Murshidabad, West Bengal, was raised in South India where his father was a civil service officer. He received a B.A. in English from Presidency College, worked as a journalist for major Kolkata newspapers and magazines, and held a residency at the Iowa Writers' Workshop in the late 1960s. In 1994, he and his wife, Meenakshi Datta (also a noted author), moved to New York to join their U.S.-born son. He now lives with the family in Queens and writes for India Abroad and other publications of the Bengali diaspora. He introduced Carolyne Wright to the work of Anuradha Mahapatra, and prepared initial English versions of many of her poems.

Mohammad Nurul Huda, born in 1949 in Cox's Bazaar, East Bengal, received his B.A and M.A. with Honours in English Literature from Dhaka University. One of Bangladesh's leading poets, he has published over three dozen volumes of poetry, fiction, essays and criticism, and anthologies of Bengali poetry. He is Director for Planning and Training of the Bangla Academy, a research institute devoted to the study and publication of Bengali language, literature, and folklore. With Carolyne Wright, he prepared initial English versions of work by several Bangladeshi women poets. He lives in central Dhaka with his family.

Syed Manzoorul Islam, born in 1951 in Sylhet, East Bengal, received a First Class First (valedictorian) B.A. and M.A. with Honours from Dhaka University, and a Ph.D. in English Literature from Queens University, Canada. Returning to Bangladesh, he has been one of the most popular and respected professors at Dhaka University ever since, serving as English Department Chair, writing (in English as well as Bengali) dozens of critical books and essays, as well as novels and journalism, and traveling abroad to speak for literary conferences and to visit his son, now an attorney in Boston. He is one of the nation's leading intellectuals and spokespersons for democracy and human rights. He lives with his wife, a social worker, in Dhaka.

Ayesha Kabir, born in 1959 in London, daughter of a Bengali father and English mother, grew up in Dhaka, where her mother died tragically during the 1971 War of Liberation. She received B.A. and M.A. in English Literature, both with highest honors, from Dhaka University, and has lived since her marriage just north of Dhaka, working as a freelance writer and translator, English language tutor, and elementary teacher. She worked with Carolyne Wright on the poems of several Bangladeshi women poets.

Sunil Baran Ray, born in 1916 in Dhaka, received a degree with Honours in Mathematics from Presidency College/University of Calcutta, served in the British and then the Indian Army during World War II, and worked until retirement as a commissioner for the Indian civil service and the Calcutta Development Authority. He has extensively translated poetry from Persian, French, and English to Bengali, and from Bengali to English, collaborating with Carolyne Wright on the work of several Kolkata women poets. He lives in south Kolkata.

Nandana (Dev) Sen, born in 1967 in Kolkata, younger daughter of Nabaneeta Dev Sen and economist Amartya Sen, studied at Presidency College and transferred to Harvard, where she received her B.A. in English, worked for a few years in academic publishing in Boston, studied directing at the University of Southern California, then was discovered by a film director while visiting her family in India. She now divides her time between Kolkata and New York, appearing in theatre and films. She worked with Carolyne Wright in Boston to translate and revise older translations of her mother's and grandmother's poems.

Carolyne Wright spent four years on Indo-U.S. Subcommission and Fulbright Senior Research fellowships in Kolkata, India, and Dhaka, Bangladesh, collecting and translating the work of Bengali women poets and writers for an anthology in progress, *A Bouquet of Roses on the Burning Ground.* For these translations, Wright has received grants and residencies from the Witter Bynner Foundation, the National Endowment for the Arts, the Seattle Arts Commission, and the Bunting Institute of Radcliffe College. She has held research associateships at Harvard University (Department of Sanskrit and Indian Studies), Wellesley College (Center for Research on Women), and Emory University (Asian Studies Program), where she also taught courses on South Asian Women's Literature which were cross-listed with English and Women's Studies.

Two volumes of translations from the Bengali are published so far, *The Game in Reverse: Poems by Taslima Nasrin* (George Braziller); and *Another Spring, Darkness: Selected Poems of Anuradha Mahapatra* (Calyx Books), work of a renowned West Bengali poet about whom Adrienne Rich has written, "across culture and language we are encountering a great world poet."

Also in progress are other individual collections of poetry by Vijaya Mukhopadhyay and Nabaneeta Dev Sen; a collection of Taslima Nasrin's essays; and Wright's own memoir about women's lives and literature in Bengal, *Crossing the Seasonal River: a Journey Among the Women of Bengal.*

Wright has also published eight books and chapbooks of poetry Her most recent collection, *A Change of Maps* (Lost Horse Press, 2006), finalist for the Idaho Prize and the Alice Fay di Castagnola Award from the Poetry Society of America, won the 2007 Independent Book Publishers Bronze Award for Poetry. Her previous book of poems, *Seasons of Mangoes and Brainfire* (Eastern Washington UP/Lynx House Books, 2nd edition 2005), won the Blue Lynx Prize, Oklahoma Book Award in Poetry, and American Book Award from the Before Columbus Foundation. At the College of Wooster in 2003-2004, Wright was Special Guest Editor for poetry for *Artful Dodge,* and she continues as Translation Editor. A visiting professor at colleges, universities, and writers' conferences around the country, she moved back to her native Seattle in 2005, where she serves on the faculty of the Whidbey Writers' Workshop MFA Program and the Richard Hugo House, and on the Board of Directors of the AWP (2004–2008).

Translation Credits

Shamim Azad, "First Love," "Conjugal Prayer," and "Sweaty Canvas." Translated by Carolyne Wright with Syed Manzoorul Islam and the author.

Sanjukta Bandyopadhyay, "Wife," and "Death Beside the Ganga." Translated by Carolyne Wright with Paramita Banerjee and the author.

Shahera Khatun Bela, "You're In My Core," and "This Blunder Wrapped in Silk." Translated by Carolyne Wright with Mohammad Nurul Huda.

Rajlakshmi Devi Bhattacharya, "Love Is Solitude" translated by Carolyne Wright with Swapna Mitra Banerjee. "Hope" translated by Carolyne Wright with Mithi Mukherjee.

Gita Chattopadhyay, "The Ritual of *Sati*." Translated by Carolyne Wright with Paramita Banerjee and the author.

Khaleda Edib Chowdhury, "Artistry in the Hair" translated by Carolyne Wright with Ayesha Kabir. "Rice Sheaves This Alluvial Night" translated by Carolyne Wright with Ayesha Kabir and A. U. M. Fakhruddin.

"Aparajita Devi" (Radharani Devi), "Sunset Colors." Translated by Carolyne Wright with Swapna Mitra Banerjee and Nandana Sen.

Nabaneeta Dev Sen, "The Temple" and "Dismissal" translated by Carolyne Wright with Paramita Banerjee, Nandana Sen, and the author. "The Swaying Lotus" translated by Carolyne Wright with Sunil B. Ray, Nandana Sen, and the author. "The Other Tongue" and "A Child's Babblings" translated by Carolyne Wright with Paramita Banerjee and the author.

Ketaki Kushari Dyson, "When There Was Land." Translated by the author.

Rama Ghosh, "What Is There to Fear." Translated by Carolyne Wright with Paramita Banerjee.

Dilara Hafiz, "Grown-Up Boy," "Mira's Hymn," and "The Majestic Night." Translated by Carolyne Wright with Syed Manzoorul Islam and the author.

Dilara Hashem, "First Sight" and "Love." Translated by Carolyne Wright and the author.

Sufia Kamal, "Love-Timid" and "That Love of Yours." Translated by Carolyne Wright with Ayesha Kabir.

Anuradha Mahapatra, "Guiltful" translated by Carolyne Wright with Jyotirmoy Datta. "Friend" and "You (I)" translated by Carolyne Wright with Paramita Banerjee.

Debarati Mitra, "He Gets Well." Translated by Carolyne Wright with Paramita Banerjee.

Vijaya Mukhopadhyay, "Companion," and "Which Floor?" Translated by Carolyne Wright with Sunil B. Ray and the author.

Taslima Nasrin, "Dark and Handsome," "Body Theory," "Divorce Letter," and "Eve Oh Eve" translated by Carolyne Wright with Mohammad Nurul Huda. "Happy Marriage" translated by Carolyne Wright with Mohammad Nurul Huda and the author. "Fire" translated by Carolyne Wright.

Ruby Rahman, "Disagreement" translated by Carolyne Wright with Syed Manzoorul Islam and the author. "This Afternoon Knows" translated by

Carolyne Wright with Syed Manzoorul Islam, Mohammad Nurul Huda, and the author.

Pratima Ray, "Marriage Vessel." Translated by Carolyne Wright with Paramita Banerjee.

Farida Sarkar, "What Love is This?" Translated by Carolyne Wright with the author.

Mallika Sengupta, "The Earth Chooses Her Own Husband," "The Blood Mark," and "The Empress's Love." Translated by Carolyne Wright with Paramita Banerjee.

Kabita Sinha, "Eve Speaks to God" translated by Carolyne Wright with the author. "You, Love" translated by Carolyne Wright with Swapna Mitra Banerjee.

Nasima Sultana, "You Said That the Map Would Be Mine" and "I'll Go Away and I Won't Say a Thing." Translated by Carolyne Wright with Mohammad Nurul Huda.

CONTINUATION OF ACKNOWLEDGMENTS FROM COPYRIGHT PAGE

"The Other Tongue" by Nabaneeta Dev Sen was quoted in part in *May You Be the Mother of a Hundred Sons: A Journey Among the Women of India*, by Elisabeth Bumiller. New York: Random House, 1990.

"The Ritual of *Sati*" by Gita Chattopadhyay, "A Child's Babblings" (as "The Child's Saying") by Nabaneeta Dev Sen, and "Companion" by Vijaya Mukhopadhyay were reprinted in *In Their Own Voice: The Penguin Anthology of Contemporary Indian Women Poets*, ed. Arlene R. K. Zide. New Delhi: Penguin India Ltd., 1993.

"Happy Marriage" by Taslima Nasrin was first published in *The New Yorker*, September 12, 1994.

Poems by Taslima Nasrin were published in *The Game in Reverse: Poems by Taslima Nasrin*. New York: George Braziller, 1995. English translations © Carolyne Wright.

Poems by Anuradha Mahapatra were published in *Another Spring, Darkness: Selected Poems of Anuradha Mahapatra*. Corvallis, Oregon: Calyx Books, 1996. English translations © Carolyne Wright.

I wish to thank the Mary Ingraham Bunting Institute of Radcliffe College, the Asian Studies Program of Emory University, the Fulbright Fellowship Program, the Indo-American Fellowship Program of the Indo-U. S. Subcommission on Education and Culture (both through the Council for International Exchange of Scholars), the Department of Sanskrit and Indian Studies of Harvard University, the Santa Fe Art Institute, the United States Information Agency, the Wellesley College Center for Research on Women, and the Witter Bynner Foundation for Poetry, for grants, fellowships, and research affiliations which made possible the undertaking and completion of this translation project and provided support and encouragement while this anthology was in progress.

COMPANIONS FOR THE JOURNEY SERIES

Inspirational work by well-known writers in a small-book format
designed to be carried along on your journey through life.